BECOME A MEDIA MAVEN

AN ENTREPRENEUR'S GUIDE TO GROWING YOUR BUSINESS WITHOUT ADS (EVEN IF YOU DON'T HAVE AN AUDIENCE) BY A TV REPORTER AND ANCHOR

CHRISTINA NICHOLSON

CHAPTER 28

Engaging in Parent Education

Parent education is a critical factor in helping caregivers understand their role in promoting children's healthy media use. Parents are in a unique position to promote a healthy infancy, they can be a reliable resource for adolescents in terms of assisting in aesthetic and moral judgments when engaging with arts and science online. Along the same lines, educational media school programs have been found to be successful in teaching children a variety of educational concepts and supporting their first- or second-language learning ability. And, of course, children learn from educational games and programs that they find interesting and that engage their attention. The goal of parent education is to help idealize children's capacity to engage the digital world.

Due to the rapid onslaught of new media forms and formats, parents are often uninformed about current understandings of children and screens. So too, policymakers need information about the impact of screen time before making decisions about adopting new policies regulating screen time in schools and in the home. To address this situation, a variety of researchers have offered recommendations and guidelines to educate parents and educators about the use of screen media by children, ranging from a list of tips for how children can use the screen; to online, evidence-based advice on constructing a Family Media Use Plan for preschoolers. However, it is unclear whether parents use evidence-based guidelines to inform their practices, or more generally how they engage with new media advisories.

CHAPTER 29

Addressing Screen Time in School Policies

In a position statement, the National Association for the Education Advancement of Young Children, the largest organization of early childhood professionals, states that while computers should have only a limited role in early childhood education - offering a minimum of only fifteen minutes of use per day, provided that is of high quality and interactive, it goes on to say that, "Technology should not replace or take time away from developmentally appropriate activities such as blocks, carpentry, dramatic play, painting, and drawing...or, most important, outdoor play in wonderful nature's classroom." Further, the National Association for the Education Advancement of Young Children has that, "Violent adult videos should not be shown to young children."

Review your school's policies and practices to help ensure that children's access to screen-based technologies in school settings does not routinely compete with opportunities for physical activity and play. Does your school or district have a screen-time policy? Does it allow for some teacher discretion in the use of screen-based devices? Or conversely, have iPads been issued to your classroom with mandated time expectations? Do computers displace recess time for students at your school? Where possible, the more traditional methods of teaching, especially in the early years, can foster much better physical and mental health. These old school ways of teaching are easier on the teacher and for most students who will later have to function in less traditional educational settings. What is beneficial for young children's physical and emotional health is also beneficial for their learning and sense of wonder about the world.

CHAPTER 30

Promoting Screen-Free Activities

C hildren are more likely to seek what they believe is important to their caregivers. For many children in this screen-saturated world, their most important caregivers find themselves more engaged in screens, talking to someone far away, or texting, checking the news and weather, social media, etc. Few parents today grew up with screen technologies, and many acknowledge at least some misgivings. Complicating all this, like earlier technologies, tablets and smartphones are so beguiling for screen users. Although spending time with a child makes many activities enjoyable, parent-child interactions also have less stimulating moments and even excruciatingly boring periods that are important for children's overall development. The struggle for a child's undivided attention can be another unpleasant side effect of screens' pull and social importance.

Many children, especially from birth to age three years, develop healthy habits from play, fun, and just being with you. With screens, those simple and important activities suffer five ways: 1) care problems for the youngest are exposed; 2) a large amount of screen use has been blamed for a lack of activity and the consequences of obesity; 3) when parents are absorbed in screens, they are less attentive to their children, have fewer conversations, and provide less emotional support; 4) and finally, 5) children learn through listening to people talk, and they learn best from people who notice what they know, do, and show interest in. Those discoveries and conversations start with care. It has also been shown that children, while using their parents' digital devices, misinterpret both their powers and screen-related parental attitudes.

CHAPTER 31

Conclusion

Second, try to understand why parents and schools are making the decisions they are. Many parents will remember rolling their eyes when their own parents told them that their music was really just 'noise'. When we understand that it's a normal part of the parent-child dynamic, we feel different about it. If we're able to say to parents, 'That's fine' rather than being judgmental, we can talk to them about screen time with an open attitude. I would argue that there's a place both for disquiet and for calm, so I think the more calm and open conversations with parents about this, the better for everyone. Third, many parents and educators look to guidelines in order to help form digital strategies. All of the guidelines we looked at take an approach to screen use of 'rules and regulations', and indeed that seems to be the predominant approach of child-Romanian guidelines. There is a problem with this because none of us is able to predict what's going to happen in screen-based media in the future. The National Institute for Health and Care Excellence, who in designing guidelines, adopted a very different mindset. They're grounded in the biological and socio-psychological effects of digital behavior and thinking, rightly believing that culture and any modern social educational settings rely on our ability to do a range of things rather than following rules.

What can we teachers do to help concerned parents with their children's screen use? We might start with these 10 suggestions. First, take a balanced view of children's screen use. There's an awful lot of scare-mongering about screens around at the moment, and much of it is to do with perpetuating 20th-century values. Most of the research around screen use is influenced by the broad principles of the Stockholm Declaration of 1952, which was primarily about guardianship and abstinence. Screen time is a hot topic right now, but actually keeping your child safe on the internet risks is part of 21st-century parenting. There are conflicting messages about screen use in general, and many parents are confused about what is good and what is bad for their children.

COMPANION WORKBOOK

Thanks so much for picking up my first book. I put together a supplemental resource for you to show my gratitude and help you get the most out of this book.

Just scan the QR code below to access the *Become a Media Maven* workbook.

You can also download it at MediaMavenAndMore.com/book.

I would like to dedicate this book to my husband, Colin. Building my business and writing this book would've been impossible without you holding down the fort and keeping our three kids happy and healthy.

INTRODUCTION

Getting attention is harder than ever now, and spending big bucks on ads seems out of reach for new business owners.

I will show you how I've helped entrepreneurs get media coverage in places like the *TODAY Show* and *Forbes* and on top podcasts . . . even though they didn't have an audience.

As a TV reporter, I received pitches from business owners, marketers, and publicists at PR agencies on a daily basis. Most of them went straight into the trash bin. It was clear the sender was clueless about the inner workings of a newsroom and what made a good, newsworthy story.

Fast forward a few years later to my new career "on the other side," and I'm able to book business owners in their dream media outlets, regardless of the size of their business, social media following, and email list or whether they have a verified social media account.

Readers of this book can achieve their vision of finally being celebrated as an expert in their industry and turn that validation into a reputable business with predictable leads and sales.

When Kylie got clear on her unique selling point, or USP, to pitch herself to be a guest on a podcast, she ended up closing a deal with a client who was persuaded by the way she articulated her value.

When Crystal landed a live, five-minute segment on TV in San Diego, not only was her zone of genius on full display to viewers in the twenty-third-largest designated market area, or DMA, in the country, but later that day, she was making deals with local brands because they perceived her as an influencer despite it being her first time being interviewed about her expertise.

You're about to hear the specific, behind-the-scenes details of those stories and many more.

With the tangible, step-by-step strategies in this book, and my tendency to overshare, together we will increase your chances of building your brand, increasing your leads, and making closing sales easier than ever by getting featured in your pie-in-the-sky goal outlets.

Right now, your competitors could be hitting send on an email that could change the trajectory of their business for years to come. Don't you want that to be you?

The publicity tips and tricks you're about to read have proven results. Each chapter provides new secrets that will help you stay top of mind with your ideal customer or client and will even give you a leg up on how to become "the media" yourself.

If you follow the formula I reveal in this book, it's highly possible you can enjoy the rest of your career with a never-ending pipeline of people who can't get enough of you.

1

HOW TO GET IN THE RIGHT MEDIA MINDSET

You might think earning exposure is designated for big brands with lots of clients or people with a team who are considered influencers, but it's not. You think that because that's the perception you have of people who are seen and heard in places like your local TV news station, your favorite podcast, or a popular website.

You think they're there because they're a big deal and, for some reason, deserve to be there. Instead, they will be a big deal *because* they're getting that media coverage. So many people get this backward—especially small business owners.

The bottom line is this: people can't do business with you if they don't know about you. This gets you known. At the same time, people will decide whether they like you. People will almost automatically trust you because you're not paying for this media coverage. Building the *know-like* trust factor has never been simpler, but it won't be easy.

Why even bother?

Why not just post on your website, schedule a bunch of social media posts, and pay for some ads? Well, you could do that . . . and as a business owner building a brand, you probably should do that. But if you focus only on the media output that you control or you pay for, your competitor will steal your spotlight.

The way to shine is to get other people who are already known, liked, and trusted to talk about you. I could go on and on about why this should be a big part of your marketing strategy, but we have a lot to get to, so let me sum it up in just three points.

It's free.

This is the best part. You don't have to pay if you're featured in the news, a guest on a podcast, mentioned online, etc. That's not to say some people won't try to charge you, but if they do, we're running into advertising territory and that's not what this is about. This is about earning media. *Earning.* It's called that for a reason.

As if I need to add a bonus to media coverage being free, how about this? It lasts forever. When you stop paying for an ad, the ad disappears. It'll no longer run on-air or online. When you are part of the content, it will last as long as the media outlet does. For example, I can still find podcasts I was a guest on nearly a decade ago just by doing a simple Google search.

It gives you instant credibility.

You gain instant credibility and authority when you're featured in a place that is known, liked, and trusted. It's like a referral or third-party endorsement.

I could get on my podcast, *Become a Media Maven*, and mention my Media Mentoring Program while I'm chatting about business growth. It's self-promotional because it's happening on my podcast. But, if you hear me on a popular business podcast, not only am I reaching an entirely new audience, but the host has essentially vouched for me by having me on his or her podcast. That's where instant credibility comes into play.

I mean, look at what happened to Dr. Oz and Dr. Phil after Oprah brought them on her show and basically said, "These are the guys I trust." Their businesses exploded.

It makes sales so much easier.

Think about your own buying behavior. When you reach out to someone cold, they usually don't want to hear from you because they think you're being self-serving, and, to be blunt, people just don't like being sold to.

On the flip side, when the leads come to you, it's because they already feel like they know you. They obviously like you, and you've earned their trust. For this reason, you can usually skip straight to the part where they sign on the dotted line because the sales conversation has already happened. It just wasn't with you one-on-one.

Let's look at this in action. I will use one of my first experiences treating myself as a client and take you from start to finish on how one podcast appearance led to tens of thousands of dollars for me, so you can grasp this concept . . . get excited about what's to come in this book so you can experience the same thing on a regular basis.

Real-life example:

When I was just one year into business, I pitched myself to be a guest on Pat Flynn's *Smart Passive Income*. I knew it was a long shot because I remembered him saying at the time that he received at least four hundred emails a week from people pitching him to be a guest on his podcast. His podcast was the first one I listened to, and I knew his audience would benefit from what I experienced being on the receiving end of so many pitches in a newsroom. So I pitched him . . . but I did it a little differently than what you'd expect.

Instead of sending Pat an email, I sent him a video. I did this because I heard him say on a podcast that despite him getting hundreds of email pitches, he almost never received videos of people pitching him to be a guest on SPI.

So I recorded a video that was less than three minutes long, uploaded it to YouTube as an unlisted video, and sent an email to Pat and his assistant with the video hyperlinked in the email. After a week or so of not hearing back, I double-checked the video views on YouTube. It had one view—and that was just me making sure everything uploaded okay.

So I sent a follow-up email, and that's what set everything in motion. To see how it unfolded, visit PodcastClout.com/Pat. There, you can see the exact email, video, and follow-up sequence that led to my being booked as a guest on *Smart Passive Income*.

From pitching to scheduling to recording to the episode going live, weeks passed. Right after the episode went live, and weeks after, my email list grew like crazy. The biggest increase was the week it went live, but I saw substantial jumps in the back end of my ConvertKit dashboard for weeks after that. ConvertKit is the software I use to collect leads and email those leads.

Fast forward a few months, and the same thing happened when I was a guest on John Lee Dumas's podcast, *Entrepreneurs on Fire* . . . but I digress. Let's get back to what happened after all those people who heard me on Pat's podcast joined my email list.

Before I get there, I have to point out how inexperienced I was as a podcast guest. I don't think I was on another podcast before this one. I had no idea what I was doing in a business space that I didn't share or even mention a freebie or lead magnet, so it's amazing I gained all those new subscribers when I didn't tell them where to go and what to do. They just took the time to figure it out because that is how powerful podcasting is.

So what happened next? I got an email from the first person to purchase my online course. Her name was Leah, and she lived on the other side of the world in Australia. Her email said, "I'm excited to finally start your course. I heard you on Pat Flynn's SPI podcast a few months back and knew instantly that I needed to do the course. It was just about signing up at the right time, which is definitely now."

Those examples are the ones that happened quickly, but remember, you also need to leverage the media you earn. I'll get to more on that later, but for now, let's keep going. The benefits from my first podcast appearance don't end there.

Over the next two years, people were sending me messages on LinkedIn telling me they found me from Pat's podcast, my email list was growing as I appeared on other podcasts (this time sharing a lead magnet), and I morphed from a freelance publicist to a public relations agency owner.

In 2018 Pat announced that he was starting his own mastermind. To join, there was an application process. Luckily for me, my name stood out among the hundreds who applied because I had been a guest on his podcast. I was one of nearly a dozen selected to join the Accelerator. I soon learned I would be joined by some of the smartest entrepreneurs I would meet. Knowing those people led to introductions to other people they knew, getting tips about speaking gigs that would lead to agency clients, and learning more about their zone of genius and how I could implement some of their tactics in my business.

After being accepted into the Accelerator, Pat invited me to be a guest on his podcast. Again. From episode 242 to episode 321, a lot changed in my business. Instead of just selling an online course and freelancing, I had a full-blown agency with a growing team of women. Like the first time, after appearing as a guest the second time, a new client came knocking . . . or DMing me on LinkedIn.

"I came across your work through the SPI podcast and was so enthusiastic about your tips and passion that I signed up for all the free stuff on your website" is what part of the message said. The message was from a man who created a product sold online. Within days, he becomes a Media Maven client paying a monthly retainer of thousands.

I could go on about the trajectory of my business stemming from that first podcast appearance, but I will wrap it up with just one more example. One year after that, in the summer of 2019, I attended Podcast Movement, the world's largest annual gathering of podcasters and the podcast industry.

Pat Flynn was leading a talk there and asked me to join him on stage to talk about my journey from podcast guest to podcast host. Just like being a guest on Pat's podcast, taking the stage with him gave me instant authority and credibility. The audience knows, likes, and trusts him, so by default, they're going to know, like, and trust me too.

And the snowball effect keeps happening, thanks to *one* appearance on *one* podcast.

Now, imagine the impact this would have on *your* business.

Stop making excuses.

What happens now when you pitch yourself? I'm guessing it's one of four things:

1. You haven't started because you don't know where to begin.
2. You don't have time because you're doing so many other things in your business.
3. You're trying. Maybe you're replying to HARO queries or pitching to be a guest on podcasts, but you're not getting a lot of responses back.
4. You're landing some coverage here and there, but it's not converting into leads or sales.

In the following chapters, we will solve those problems. First, I need to address the elephant in the room, which I honestly didn't even know existed until I started working with small business owners in my Media Mentoring Program.

Imposter syndrome.

I think we all have an idea of what this is, but something that caught me by surprise was one part of the definition.

Imposter syndrome is loosely defined as doubting your abilities and feeling like a fraud. It disproportionately affects high-achieving people, who find it difficult to accept their accomplishments.

It's that second sentence that blew my mind a bit. To take the research on this topic even further, one study found that about 70 percent of all people have felt like an imposter at some point. Imposter syndrome often affects those who are highly capable perfectionists.

Again, the second part.

Because this is something that holds a lot of people back and, in my experience, is the leading reason people don't put in an effort to earn media exposure, we're going to squash it right now. Because if we don't, the rest of this book won't do you any good because you won't implement what's in it.

Here are five things to know about imposter syndrome:

You're probably more talented than you think.

A negative belief you may have is that you're a fraud and it's only a matter of time until the luck runs out and you're exposed. It's an unconscious refusal to assign credit appropriately. This is a belief and not reality.

Another negative belief you may notice is that when more wins and accomplishments pile up, you aren't able to clear the cobwebs and look at your achievements for what they really are. They really are high-performance.

On my podcast, *Become a Media Maven*, lifestyle journalist Alice Dubin said, "Many people are underselling themselves, especially women, because they don't feel like they've earned the right to take up a lot of space," she said. "We do know what we're talking about. You have to announce yourself as an expert."

Finally, consider this. If a stranger shared your accomplishments with you as their own, would the logical conclusion be that they are all a stroke of luck and therefore a fraud? Probably not. So, if you wouldn't treat someone else's achievements like that, then why do it to yourself? (That's not a rhetorical question. Seriously ask yourself that question and answer it.)

You're cursed with knowledge.

The curse of knowledge, or knowledge blindness, is when you've learned something and have known it for so long (and so well) that you can't imagine other people not knowing it. This is an extremely important component of impostor syndrome.

Remember that the information you're familiar with is not always common knowledge. You know more than you think you do.

Whenever I start thinking what I know is second nature to someone, I think of what is so over my head that even the 101 version has me lost—things like how the stock market works, NFTs, and cryptocurrency.

On my podcast, *Become a Media Maven*, independent journalist Kelsey Ogletree said, "I would love to hear from more small business owners. I don't think writers hear from those kinds of people enough, and I'm someone who wants to champion those smaller brands, but a lot of times we just don't hear about them. If you're a business that has never been featured in the media and you think you're too small, that's gold for me. If no one's written about you, my editor's going to love it."

The stuff you don't know? They don't either.

The amount of knowledge available to us is unlimited and growing. Things get more complicated and complex by the day. It's impossible to keep up . . . and that's okay.

Stop worrying about what you do and don't know—and stop believing you should know it all.

Instead, think about how you approach not knowing something. Focus on curiosity, diligence, and your ability to figure things out. Those are the things that will determine your success.

Ponder your accomplishments.

Again, ask yourself: *If a stranger shared these accomplishments with me, would the logical conclusion be that they are all a stroke of luck and therefore a fraud?*

Content manager and online contributor Jessica Lawlor was a guest on my podcast, *Become a Media Maven*, and advised small business owners to "Get started where you are. If you have a business or you're passionate about something, you can write about it or you can speak about it."

Take the time to review your accomplishments and celebrate how far you have come. Look back. Be good to yourself. Smile when you see the upward trajectory of your career.

Make this a quarterly or biannual commitment to yourself. Put a reminder in your calendar right now. You'll begin to see that you are truly worthy of praise and the label *high performer*.

There is a snowball effect.

The interesting thing about impostor syndrome is that when you finally beat it (or contain it), you're able to view your own career through more of an external lens.

That's when you're able to believe in yourself, and when you look back on all you've done, you will feel really satisfied. You'll no longer believe you're lucky. Instead, you will know the effort and energy you put into what you do has resulted in great wins.

Those beliefs and that confidence snowball to create an unstoppable force of positive energy that helps you achieve things you never thought were possible. That's when you start really winning.

Take action.

Now, I need you to commit to taking action on what you're going to learn in the rest of this book. Knowledge is not power. It's potential power. It becomes powerful only when you do something with it, so my challenge to you is to do something with the knowledge you gain on these pages. Make that commitment to yourself and to me before moving on to chapter 2.

Send me a message on social media at @ChristinaAllDay and tell me you're committed to executing what's in this book.

2

IT'S ALL ABOUT YOU

Now that we have our mind right, let's build the foundation for everything that makes this work. It's you.

Simply put, your personal brand captures who you are and what skills you bring to the table. In turn, it helps you make powerful connections and leads to new opportunities. In this case, those opportunities are getting coverage online, on TV, in print, on podcasts, and on social media.

I taught personal branding for publicity on day one of my three-day bootcamp, Pitch Publicity Profit.

On day two, one of the boot campers, Kylie, posted in the Facebook group, "I signed a new client! It just made today that much sweeter."

While this specific messaging is designed to pique the interest of journalists, editors, bookers, podcast hosts, and influencers, it also clarifies who you are, what you do, and why you're different from your competition—so naturally, it's ideal for bringing in leads and closing sales.

Your unique selling point or proposition, also known as your USP, is what makes you better than someone else who does the same thing you do.

The key here is to get as specific as possible. I can't emphasize that enough. If your one- to two-sentence USP does not answer the question *Why me?* Then you will miss many of the shots you take at landing a podcast interview, quote online, or TV segment.

Let's talk specifics.

While this first exercise may seem like Business 101, please humor me and fill in the blanks:

> I help *(insert ideal client) (insert how you help)* so that *(insert ideal client's outcome)*.

Another way of doing this without the "I help" starter would be:

> I am *(insert what you're fabulous at)* for *(insert ideal client—if you didn't mention them already)* so that *(insert ideal client's outcome)*.

I'm not just going to share this and leave you hanging, because even with this one-sentence template, people are still too vague, and it doesn't do them any good. Before I break down how to get even more specific than you probably are right now, answer the following about your ideal client:

1. Age:
2. Gender:
3. Location:
4. Position:
5. Conferences they attend:

6. People they follow on social media:
7. Podcasts they listen to:
8. Websites they visit:

If you need help answering some of these questions, think of your best customers or clients. If you're still new to business and haven't had too many, then think of your dream customers or clients.

Let me share some examples of generic USPs and how we can make them much better by being more specific:

> I help *(business owners) (with website creation)* so that *(they convert more prospects online)*.

Now, this isn't terrible, but it could be so much better, like:

> I help *(women service providers) (capture leads on their website)* so that *(they collect emails from 20 percent of their website visitors)*.

Which person are you more likely to hire? To book an interview with? To listen to on a podcast? Probably the second one because it's much clearer.

Let's try one more:

> I help *(experts) (book more speaking gigs)* so that *(they sell more programs)*.

Instead, break it down further, like this:

> I help *(nonfiction authors) (get paid six figures to speak on stages)* so that *(they sell 10x more books AND 3x more programs at every talk)*.

Again, if you were an expert who happened to be a nonfiction author, which one of these would you gravitate toward?

Don't be afraid you might pigeonhole yourself to this one sentence for life. You can change it depending on who you're reaching out to. In one pitch, you could swap out *nonfiction authors* for *aspiring speakers* and drop the *sell 10x more books*.

For example, when I pitch myself to be a guest on podcasts, sometimes I say, "I help *(nonfiction authors) (book interviews on top podcasts),*" and other times I'll say, "I help *(women service providers) (land contributing roles on popular websites).*"

You can, and should, have a few different versions of these statements depending on who the audience is. The more niche, the better. Later in this chapter, I will share more of what I send when I pitch myself.

Many times, I post media opportunities my colleagues are working on in the private Facebook group for my Media Mentoring Program clients. Before they even pass along the questions they want to be answered for the articles they're working on, they want to know two things: what's your expertise and why you. That's why this exercise is so crucial.

Now, let's take this a step further. This next exercise is vital because it's what every single member of the media will ask before deciding whether they will choose to feature you in a story. This will also help you write an amazing two- to three-sentence bio to include at the end of every pitch you send.

Yes, we have more blanks to fill in:

1. What are you great at?
2. Why are you great at it?
3. Why are you the only person to talk to about this?
4. What proof or results do you have to show?

5. Why should I (the receiver of the information) care?

Just like before, some of these points may change depending on who you're talking to, especially the last *Why should I care?* Part.

Let's use me as an example to address number three above. I use two things that make me different from everyone else teaching about media and public relations on the internet:

1. I used to work as a TV reporter and anchor, so I know what happens in a newsroom and in those morning and afternoon meetings as we decided what to cover and why. Having been on the receiving end of pitches from PR agencies, marketers, and business owners is invaluable.
2. I have been known to hold nothing back and overshare. Contrary to what many internet experts say, I don't make people pay for the *how*. If it comes up in conversation or they ask, I share.

I honestly believe when it comes to bettering ourselves personally or professionally, we already know everything we need to do. We just need someone there to help us *while* we execute.

Take the goal of having a body like Britney Spears in her "I'm A Slave 4 U" days. We all know we need to eat healthy and work out, but it's hard to do on our own, so we pay for the food, meal plans, gym membership, trainers, etc. to make it happen.

This is what part of my podcast pitch looks like, word for word. (I told you I have no problem oversharing.)

Your audience will benefit from the tangible takeaways, as I transparently break down:

1. How one podcast appearance led to tens of thousands of dollars
2. How I landed a three-minute segment on the *TODAY Show* for a startup
3. How I got Amy Porterfield her first TV segment on CNN Headline News
4. Why the scams in your DMs are too good to be true when it comes to landing media exposure
5. How promoting myself on LinkedIn led to an invitation to do a TED Talk in Boca Raton

Four out of these five points are very specific to me and my experience. No one can take these talking points and use them as their own. That's what makes them work and makes other people want to know more.

While the fourth point may not be as specific as the reset, and it's not something I hear a lot of experts and thought leaders talk about, I know it's something a lot of people experience. Plus, nothing drives me crazier than those faux PR agencies taking advantage of new business owners and giving the industry a bad name.

Take action

As my mentor and BFF from afar Oprah Winfrey says, I hope this chapter gave you an *aha moment*. It's important to grasp this foundation before moving on to the next chapter.

Before moving on, fill in the blanks with as much detail as you possibly can. If you're interested in working with me to craft your USP, it's what happens on day one of my bootcamp Pitch Publicity Profit. Check it out at MediaMavenAndMore.com/publicity.

3

STOP WRITING PRESS
RELEASES—IT'S NOT 1990

ARE you ready to start moving through the Media Maven process even more? In the last chapter, we laid the groundwork for a strong foundation. Now, it's time to build the damn thing!

You're going to learn how to do this from someone who did not go to college for public relations. Trust me, that's a good thing. I've heard what they're *still* teaching students who want to get into the industry. It's very outdated.

I'm coming from a place of experience but not in PR. Instead, my experience is from being on the receiving end of thousands of pitches in a variety of TV newsrooms.

Hi! I'm Christina.

Anyone can create a course on the internet, start a podcast, and write a book. So I think it's a good time to introduce myself.

After graduating with a degree in public affairs journalism from The (yes, The) Ohio State University, I applied for job after job for nearly two years. I'm really going to date myself with this story, but imagine this:

I sat in my apartment with a DVD in one hand and a blank VHS tape in the other. I used a dual DVD/VHS VCR to copy what was on the DVD to the VHS. For those of you who are younger than us millennials, a VCR was a video cassette recorder. After copying my resume tape to a VHS, I'd pop a label on it and mail it to every single TV station hiring a TV reporter in the country.

It took me quite a few months to get my first job offer. It was a reporting job in Dennison, Texas, and it paid about ten dollars an hour. For context, this was around 2005.

At that time, I was making much more than that working as a server and bartender at Rooster's in German Village. So I was quick to turn down that job. What I didn't know at the time was it would be two years before I got the next job offer.

Here is the thing about college. Sometimes the people teaching you about the thing you want to do have never actually done that thing. For that reason, they have no idea what to prepare you for. In school, I never learned how to apply for TV jobs, how to create a resume tape, how competitive the industry is, or how little on-camera talent got paid.

Thankfully, I had an internship at the local ABC and FOX affiliate. I remember having conversations with reporters like Maria Durant, Shannon McCormick, and Anne Allred (a fellow Buckeye) about these things. Because I knew I was going to be working more and making less money when I started my TV career, I sent out tapes during the day, worked at night, and saved most of my money.

I took a month-long internship at News 12 The Bronx. There, I drove a Prius around the Big Apple; carried my own tripod, camera, and microphone to sites; and shot, wrote, and edited my own stories. I would leave for work so early in the morning that it was dark, take the subway an hour and a half to a bus station, then take the bus to the TV station on Soundview Avenue. I'd return the same way after dinner in the dark.

By the way, I stayed in a rented room I found listed on Craigslist. I know. I have no idea how I'm still alive either.

But that's where I made my next tape, which led to my second job offer in 2007. Immediately, I said yes and agreed to work in Beaumont, Texas, for twelve dollars an hour.

I made great friends, met my future Canadian husband at a country bar, and put together a new résumé tape to get the hell out of there. But before I could start sending it out to see what new place I'd land next, my boyfriend, who played hockey for the ECHL, was being sent to play for a team in Fort Myers, Florida. So the plan was to move there with him and get a TV job there.

I was intimidated by approaching news directors in the Fort Myers market. At the time, it was ranked number 64 out of 212, and I was coming from a station ranked number 141. It would be a big jump for a reporter. Still, I applied to the three stations in the market.

Think about that for a second. That's how competitive this industry is. In the entire area of Fort Myers, which includes Marco Island, Naples, Port Charlotte, and more, there are only three TV stations. Each one employed about ten reporters. That's thirty jobs in total. When one job would open up, a news director would get hundreds of applicants.

I like to say I harassed the news directors at all the stations until one hired me. I remember one day I was laying at the pool with some of the "hockey wives" when the assistant news director from WINK, the CBS station, called and said, "Christina, we give up. We'll talk to you."

I worked at WINK for about two years. I made about $28,000 a year there. This was in 2008–2010, so no, it's not impressive, but the goal in TV is to keep working your way up to eventually make the big bucks. But how much longer did I need to work those wild hours with no lunch breaks and beyond rude viewer emails before it's worth it?

Long story short, I ended up getting fired for having a side hustle. I tell that story on my podcast (along with the two other times I've been fired). That should've been the first sign I was made to be an entrepreneur. I wouldn't be a business owner for another four years though. First, I needed to finish my TV career in one of the best TV markets in the country, Miami.

Working in the Miami and Fort Lauderdale market was a huge jump. For context, when I worked there until 2014, it was the sixteenth-largest TV market in the country. I worked for the NBC station that was owned and operated by the NBC network. I finally felt like I made it.

Then, the industry changed.

The awful emails and social media messages were expected, but in a bigger market, they became more frequent. For example, I have a Google folder of death threats I received for weeks after reporting on the drag racing arrest of Justin Bieber. Holy smokes! Those Beliebers are something.

Outside of the passionate Beliebers, you had people who believe *the media* were *the enemy* and would yell at you, chase you, and even get physical with you just for doing your job. Once, I was standing in front of the camera seconds away from going live and a man walked up to me and punched me in the side so hard that I almost fell over. Because I was seconds away from going live, I had no choice but to stand face-forward and wait for my cue to go live.

The competitiveness of the industry was getting worse. Working at a cable station in New York City, it wasn't surprising to hear of journalists working as one-man bands, but in Miami, this was new.

I remember knocking on a sex offender's door while I was nine months pregnant, by myself, with a camera in one hand and microphone in the other hand, trying to get an interview with him because he just bonded out of jail.

I once had a woman in the newsroom, who also happened to be my co-anchor, turn on me when I anchored a show solo while she was out.

I nearly fell asleep on my drive home from work after the 11:00 p.m. news multiple times when my daughter was just a few months old. (I tried telling my Canadian husband that an employer paying for ten weeks of maternity leave was actually a great deal in the United States. FYI, Canadians get paid maternity leave for a year and a half. Oh yeah, and they can split it with their partner.)

I had an image consultant tell me we would get more viewers if I parted my hair a tad more to the left.

I stood in hurricanes for hours telling people it was rainy and windy. There really is only so much to say when you get to the eighth hour of wall-to-wall storm coverage.

I could go on and on with the stories that are borderline unbelievable, but that's not for this book. (Maybe the next one?)

After spending most days and nights outside of a crime scene and rushing to drop off my kids or pick them up from daycare, it was time for a change. By this point, I think you know what that change was. That's the short story long about how I got into PR.

I thought publicists were annoying AF.

Let's bring this full circle into how all of that makes me qualified to tell you how to get more attention in the media without spending money on ads.

Things are different at every station, but one constant was the morning meeting at 9:30 a.m. and the afternoon meeting at 2:30 p.m. This is where the producers, reporters, and assignment managers joined together to talk about three things:

1. **What do we need to cover?** This includes stories we covered in the previous newscasts that need to be followed up on or new stories that are breaking locally or nationally.
2. **What is on the calendar?** Tons of pitches are sent to the newsroom; if they have a date tied to them or some kind of urgency, they will be brought up on the appropriate day.
3. **What do you have to pitch?** For me, this was the most anxiety-inducing part of the job. The smaller the market, the more creative you have to get with story ideas—because when points number one and number two fail, it's all on you as the reporter to fill time in the newscast.

In all three of these cases, business owners of all sizes or their publicists send emails to try to get coverage; they want to be included in the news of the day, get on the newsroom calendar, or pique a reporter's interest with an enterprise story.

What does it mean to enterprise a story? These kinds of stories are when a reporter gets creative and comes up with a newsworthy idea. In this chapter, you will learn about a few successful real-life examples.

The problem? Most of the pitches sent to the newsroom did not even make it to a discussion in the morning or afternoon meetings. They were *that* bad. The purpose of this chapter is to share my perspective from being in the newsroom so you aren't like all the publicists who drove me nuts.

For some reason, certain people think it's the media's job to promote them as if they are entitled to coverage or *a free commercial*. I'm not sure where this idea comes from, but it's there. Sometimes this thought process is delivered subtly, and other times it's blunt and rude.

Most of the time, this attitude would stem from a bad pitch. So what makes a bad pitch? A pitch that is long, boring, and overly promotional is the norm.

Then, on the off chance that I would respond, the publicist making suggestions on how I should put the story together and what I should say in my script is what really irked me. At the time, I would think, *Who does this person think she is telling me how to do my job?* I would smile and nod politely while doing my best to move things along and make it a much smaller production than the client's PR representative thought it was.

Now, as the owner of a PR agency, I'm not excusing that behavior, but I am seeing it through a different lens. Earning clients coverage is hard. As someone working to earn attention in an outlet you don't own and aren't paying, the pressure is on to show your client success. Plus, I've learned many clients of PR agencies have unrealistic expectations due to the agency overpromising things they shouldn't and a lack of education on how the industry works. Then, there is that entitlement part I mentioned.

Still, coming into the situation with an overbearing or pushy attitude doesn't do you or your client any favors. As someone trying to earn coverage for yourself or a client, you have one job.

Make the reporter's job as easy as possible.

If you do that, you will get the promotion you seek by default. It will be a wonderful side effect of contributing the resources you had available to bring a story to publish.

I remember once I replied to a pitch I was sent to my email address at WTVJ, the NBC station in Miami. I called around 10:00 a.m. and asked whether we could come out to do an interview and shoot some B-roll (TV talk for video). The person on the other end replied in a frantic, "We're not ready. We're not ready. Please give us one or two weeks to prepare." This person was not making my job easy. So I covered something else that day, and that business never got the attention they sought because they didn't understand how TV news worked when they hit *Send*.

Ugh, press releases.

Do you like that chapter title? At the time I'm writing this, it's what's on the homepage of my website at MediaMavenAnd-More.com.

I already mentioned the wrong way to pitch: with something long, boring, and overly promotional. Most of the time, this is what press releases look like. I remember when I worked at a PR agency for six months after leaving the TV news industry and asked why press releases ended with *** at the bottom center. I was told that was to let the journalist know the press release was done. I thought that was what periods were for.

Besides the wild punctuation to end something, I remember watching a documentary on Netflix called *Conversations with a Killer: The Ted Bundy Tapes*. In the documentary, a member of law enforcement was interviewed about how they were making the public aware that this killer was on the run from state to state. He said they were sending out press releases to spread the word.

Keep in mind that this was in the late 1970s and early '80s. It's absolutely wild to me that people think that something common-place in media and communications in the late '70s and early '80s is the go-to method to spread the word today.

Not to mention, if you speak to anyone in a newsroom, they will tell you the last thing they need is another press release in their inbox. Most of the time, people in a newsroom are on the receiving end of one email sent to hundreds of people at the same time.

At the end of 2022, Dan Kois wrote an article for *Slate* magazine titled: "My PR Day of Yes: I Accepted Every Publicist Pitch I Got for a Full Day. If Only I Knew What I'd Done."

Part of the article reads:

"The fact that I'm receiving all these pitches in the first place suggests that many, many publicists send out press emails blindly, to every email address they can buy, shotgunning them into the media world in hopes that just one might hit its target."

Press releases distribution services. Ugh, again.

In all five newsrooms I worked in, I never looked at the wires. The *newswire* or *wire* is a feed of press releases that people pay to distribute to journalists and newsrooms across the world.

I'm sure sending something across the wire worked great many years ago, but today, there aren't too many earth-shattering things happening there. If there were, we wouldn't find out about it in a small window on the left side of our screen that's always updating. Instead, it'd be news in our inbox.

I've written press releases and have paid hundreds of dollars to have them distributed because it's what a client insisted on. On the surface, the results looked great. The press release was picked up by hundreds of news outlets—some of them top tier, like MSNBC. Then, the service I paid sent an email with all the links and a positive message to drive the point home that if we pay them money, we will get big-time coverage.

But there are some problems here that they don't tell you.

First, a news article was never really written. Instead, the press release was copied and pasted, word for word.

Second, no one can really find the press release. When I've done this for clients in the past, I'll go to the website and search the home page and different sections for the *news*, and I can never find it. So I use the search bar to type in keywords in hopes of finding the press release that's made it onto the site. Nothing. Unless you have the obnoxiously long URL that takes you to the hidden section of the website that shows your press release copied and pasted, no one is going to see it.

Third, there is no search engine optimization incentive. At the very least, you could include a hyperlink in the press release and get those backlinks from websites with high domain authority, right? Wrong. One of two things will happen. The links will be marked as no-follow because you're paying for placement, or the press release distribution service you're hiring will create a masked email and backlink for their own tracking purposes.

I've heard business owners tell me they know all this but pay for these services anyway because it's guaranteed coverage and they can put the impressive logos on their website *as featured* for credibility. Honestly, I don't think that works like it used to. Instead of the logo, I want to see the story. If the story is a copied-and-pasted press release, not too many people are going to be impressed.

In other words, there are better ways to pitch. Let's get to what to do instead.

Take action.

Say this with me: "I will not write a long, boring press release to try to get media coverage."

4

HIT A HOME RUN WITH YOUR PITCH

A REPORTER DOESN'T NEED to know a lot to decide whether or not a story is worth pursuing—just like you don't need to know a lot to decide whether you're going to read it, watch it, or listen to it.

Let's build your first media list.

When it comes to building a media list, or a list of media prospects to pitch, don't fall into the trap of adding outlets because they sound cool. Could *Good Morning America* work wonders for your business if you were featured? Maybe, but not always.

Let's use one of my first clients as an example to demonstrate the importance of focusing on what your audience is consuming instead of getting distracted with the big-name TV shows, websites, and publications.

Right after I left TV news, I was on the hunt for small business owners looking for PR help on LinkedIn and Upwork (eLance at the time). That's where I found a man with a running app who wasn't getting anywhere with the latest press release they were pitching. (I'll share more on that later in this chapter.)

The founder of the running app wanted to target runners, and he had his eye on the prize. His dream outlet was *Runner's World*, a magazine and website with running news, training advice, inspiring stories, running shoe reviews, gear tips, and more. The audience was a perfect fit!

Before landing coverage in *Runner's World*, the founder told his story on local TV in Washington, DC, where he lived, and in the *Washington Post*. That article was picked up by the *Chicago Tribune*. Shortly after, a producer from the *TODAY Show* called and wanted to tell the founder's story.

It wasn't until months later that a pitch I sent to *Runner's World* landed. Then, runners from around the world had the opportunity to learn more about the app, why it was created, and how to use it.

I'm so glad this startup founder understood the goal of earning media coverage isn't just to look cool. Sure, sharing a three-minute segment that aired on *TODAY* is pretty damn impressive, but there's a lot of people who watch national morning TV and don't enjoy running.

The point is different media outlets can do different things for your brand.

For example, if you have a brick-and-mortar location, getting coverage on and in the local news and partnering with local content creators and influencers is where you will see the biggest growth.

If you have an online business and want to build your email list, then being a guest on podcasts will move the needle for you.

With that in mind, let's start building a media list with the right kind of media contacts.

First, open a spreadsheet. (I like to use Google sheets.) Then, you're going to create ten columns:

1. Industry Topic
2. Name
3. Email Address
4. Media Outlet
5. Website
6. Social Media Handle & Link
7. Pitching Dates
8. Pitching Notes
9. Links
10. Misc.

In the fourth column, Media Outlet, brain-dump your dream media outlets. Based on what you just learned, your dream outlet may have changed, so remember to choose where you want to be seen based on your end goal.

A tip to do this is to hop online and search your industry topic + news, podcasts, websites, etc. For example, when I search marketing + podcasts, I'm instantly served dozens of popular marketing podcasts.

There are a few other ways you can find this information:

- Go to the media outlet's website and check out the pages like contact, about us, news team, etc.
- Search keywords on social media, like LinkedIn and Twitter/X.
- Find previous, relevant articles online and follow the writer's link to their contact information.

You can time-block doing this and handle it yourself, hire a virtual assistant to fill in the blanks, or purchase software to do this, like Podcast Clout if podcasts are your focus.

To save time and money and get further faster, time-batch filling out your spreadsheet with media outlets and contacts that scream quality over quantity.

Keep it short and sweet.

In the last chapter, I told you why press releases are antiquated. Now, I'm going to show you what to send instead.

Your pitch should have five components.

1. Let the person receiving the email know why they are getting it. Not the pitch, the person.

So many PR agencies blast the same email to five hundred people at the same time. Not only is this terrible, it's too common. To stand out, let the person know why you chose *them* to email. Say something personal about your connection to their beat (what they cover), something they tweeted/posted about last week, or the fact that you both went to the same college.

2. Pitch your story idea.

Our inboxes are busy places, so you need to get right to the point. This is where people fall flat because they get too self-serving and promotional. You need to ensure your story is both newsworthy and timely. Don't worry. I'll cover more on this later.

3. Share talking or visual points.

You need to give the podcast host an idea of how the conversation will go. You need to let the TV producer know you can offer visuals. Make sure you are offering them something they've never heard or seen before.

4. Why you?

Now, you can be promotional . . . kinda. Tell them why you are the person they should talk to about the topic you just pitched. Could they go to your competitor or an advertiser with the idea and they step in the role? I hope not! Prove to them you are the one for the interview, segment, or feature.

5. Tell them what is in it for them.

It blows my mind how many people will earn media exposure and do nothing with it. Not only is that terrible PR, but it really bothers journalists. Let them know that you will share the coverage with your audience after you give them everything they need to make it happen.

Then, you will end with your contact information and be available at the drop of a hat, because if you're not, they will go to your competition for the story. Many times, members of the media won't wait for what's best. They have to take what comes first.

If you want to see the exact pitch one of my Media Mentoring Program clients used to get booked on live TV using this formula, visit ExactPitch.com.

Timing is everything.

In the last section, I mentioned making your pitching timely in my second point. If you don't give a member of the media a reason to cover the story *now*, then they will put it on the back burner and eventually forget about it.

Here are some things to keep in mind that will put an expiration date on your pitches:

1. The calendar

Focusing on awareness days like Mother's Day, Amazon Prime Day, or National Mac and Cheese Day will help give your stories that timely angle.

In the spring, I pitched online course creator Amy Porterfield to CNN Headline News. The program was called "On the Story" and was hosted by Lynn Smith at the time. The focus of my idea was that high school graduates didn't need to follow a traditional route to college. Instead, they could purchase an online course and learn everything they need to build a successful career.

The producer and host loved the online course angle but wanted to air the segment the Friday before Mother's Day, so the segment was tweaked to cover how moms can make money at home by creating their own online course.

When you look at the calendar, you don't just get timely story ideas, but you create a sense of urgency to tell the story before it's too late.

2. The seasons

Like days on the calendar, seasons give you timeliness but a tad more flexibility.

For example, around New Year's, you can expect to see more health and wellness topics infiltrate the news cycle. During the summer, there are more travel stories. From Thanksgiving until the end of the year, it's gift guide season. If you have a product that sells online, you can find a gift guide for it!

3. National news

If something is trendy nationally, then you should be able to find a local angle for it.

I remember a day when I was working as a reporter at NBC in the Miami and Fort Lauderdale market around the time Cory Monteith, an actor from *Glee*, died of a heroin overdose. I localized that story by talking to a doctor who was an addiction specialist.

He didn't talk about the entertainment industry. Instead, he gave his expertise on drug addiction, the drug making a comeback from the 1980s, and more.

4. Local news

When something is already happening in your area, you could offer another angle to that story as a potential follow up.

For example, a story about the local housing market and people being "priced out of paradise" could be followed up with an interview from a real estate agent on the five steps buyers can take to find an affordable home or an interior designer on the three things you can do to make your current home a better fit for your family.

Seal the deal.

A member of the media has the tough job of doing two things at once: educate and entertain. One thing that makes this a slam dunk is emotion. That means you need to include emotion in your story.

There were so many times when a doctor or health professional would pitch a story but they didn't have what we called a *real person* to go along with it. For example, a doctor could have a great idea to talk about the sudden craze of people using semaglutide injections to lose weight. Sure, that's educational, but it won't be entertaining unless we have the patient or real person telling their story. That's where the emotion comes into play.

When I worked with a local nonprofit that helped kids fighting cancer by creating experiences for them, like golf outings and summer camps, I knew I needed more than just the founder to be available. So every interview I booked included a local child who benefited from the organization to tell their story. Otherwise, it would've been much harder to seal the deal.

Help a Reporter Out.

Some may call HARO, or Help a Reporter Out, easy low-hanging fruit for media coverage, but it's not . . . anymore. I have a love/hate relationship with the website.

HARO connects journalists to experts they can quote for a story. If you sign up as a source, you will receive three emails throughout the day with queries from them to respond to.

Years ago, this worked like gangbusters for experts looking to get coverage. Since the website was acquired by a marketing company, things have changed.

The biggest problem with HARO today is that anyone can claim they are a journalist and post anything. For example, during the holidays, so-called bloggers will post that they're putting together a gift guide on the best tech gifts for teens, but their goal isn't to write a helpful Christmas shopping article. Instead, it's to collect as many tech gadgets as publicists are willing to send.

Sometimes "journalists" will wait until you respond to just turn around and try to sell you an advertisement, and other times you are one of hundreds of people responding to a query.

However, you can have luck with the platform. In 2022 my friend Amy Landino, a YouTuber niched in productivity, responded to a HARO query posted anonymously. A few days later, she sat on stage with Tamron Hall on the *Tamron Hall Show* talking about the business of influencing.

So does it work? Yes, it can. You just need to know what to look out for to ensure you're not getting scammed . . . and if not, you need to know how to stand out from the hundreds of others just like you who are responding to the same query.

Here are some ways you can stand out when you respond to a HARO query:

1. Use the HARO summary as the subject line in your email.

By copying and pasting the poster's own words and putting it in the subject line, there is no confusion as to what is inside the email. This will set you apart from everyone else responding who may not appear as organized as you.

2. Address the person by their first name.

Unless this person posted anonymously, there is no reason why you shouldn't get personal.

3. Use the HARO email to respond.

It will redirect to their personal or professional email. If the journalist responds to your email, you will have their direct email address. This is helpful in following up or pitching future stories.

4. Be mindful of the deadline.

With HARO, it's first come, first served. That's why it's important to check your email right after the emails go out in the morning, afternoon, and evening if you're going to make responding to queries a PR strategy.

5. Just answer their questions.

Give the journalists exactly what they want—no more and no less. It's shocking how many people completely ignore the query and go into a self-serving promotional pitch. I remember once I posted as a journalist looking for a source on a specific topic and once of the responses I got was from a person promoting their book that had nothing to do with my query.

6. Do not send attachments.

If you send attachments, the email may not be sent and will be stuck in . . . where ever emails get stuck.

7. Answer the question *Why you?*

Sound familiar? This is the part where you say why you are the perfect source for this story. Your unique selling point, or USP, is crucial in both pitching and responding to members of the media. It can also help you land speaking gigs and book deals, so perfect it!

8. Offer an incentive.

End the email with "Please let me know if you use this in your story. I'd love to share it with my audience online." Sharing a journalist's work is so important for you as a business owner and them as a journalist. With so much emphasis on clicks and engagement, this is how you say thank you to the person giving you time and space on their platform.

9. Finally, set up a Google alert for your name and your business name. Many times, no one will let you know what is running and when it's running. Many writers who contribute to websites don't even know when things will publish and what the final edit will look like. Without the alert, you may miss amazing publicity you earned.

Take action.

Take a look at the calendar you use and work backward to plan on booking coverage for the future. This doesn't just serve as a reminder of what to pitch when, but it can also act as a content calendar to keep you ahead of the game on your blog and social media.

5

______

SPEAK UP!

SSOMETIMES IT'S important to take things into your own hands, isn't it? In the last chapter, you learned how members of the media can help increase your exposure by including you in their work. Now, you're going to learn how to become a member of the media in order to have more control over your message while still earning that valuable third-party endorsement.

Become a contributor.

If you enjoy creating content, becoming a regular online contributor is one of the best things you can do to build your personal brand. Instead of pitching yourself or waiting for an opportunity that is a fit, you can have a regular role of publishing articles based on your expertise on a weekly basis.

But first, don't pay to play.

Before I get into the steps of becoming a contributor, I'm going to advise you do not pay to become a contributor. Because people don't pay attention to ads like they used to, brands are getting creative about how they advertise.

For example, platforms like *Forbes*, *Entrepreneur*, and *Rolling Stone* have started to charge people to contribute. They'll disguise this as a great opportunity to become a member and call the platform you contribute to part of a "council" or "network" to make you believe it's an honor you've been accepted into this exclusive membership.

At the end of the day, they're collecting money from you to promote yourself in the form of you creating content for them. Not only is this sales process very disingenuous, but many aspects of it don't work for you as they would if you were a true contributor.

When you pay for coverage like this, you are not earning authority and credibility. People are wising up to these pay-to-play tactics, and it can work against you. In an episode on my podcast *Become a Media Maven*, I shared a quote from a member of the media who said in part:

"The thing I dislike about it is when someone that's part of Forbes Council claims they were 'featured in *Forbes*' or 'writes for *Rolling Stone*' as if it were earned. That's when I think less of them. So many lists and memberships are P2P that I take all of them with a grain of salt. Thirty Under 30? Don't care. You put your head down and do great work? I care A LOT."

In addition to this, the hyperlinks in the articles may be no-follow links and won't contribute to that site's ranking because the coverage is paid for.

Start small.

It's nearly impossible to land a contributing role at a media outlet without some samples or examples of previously published work.

This is another reason it's important to showcase your expertise in places like your own blog or on your LinkedIn page. You can also use other platforms that accept contributors without a backlog of published work, like Medium and Thrive Global. They key here is to have a place to send editors to see what you're capable of.

Pitch yourself.

Then, it's time to decided where you want to publish your expertise. I've made it easy for you to start. Just visit 16Places.com for sixteen places that are accepting contributors. There, you can find the high-quality websites, pitch ideas, and the contact information of the people to reach out to for the opportunity.

If those sixteen places aren't a fit for your niche, then head to your favorite search engine and type in whatever media outlet you want to contribute to or the niche you want to write about or target + "contributor" or "online contributor" etc.

When you have an idea of where you want to contribute, I suggest pitching a recurring theme instead of an idea for just one article. This increases your chances of earning coverage on a regular basis and it also lets the editor at the media outlet know you're in it for the long haul.

Sometimes, you can get paid for the articles you write. It just depends on the media outlet. If not, don't brush it off as "working for free." This is why it's vital to ensure that the coverage you will earn as a contributor is geared toward your ideal customer or client. Remember, we want to turn this publicity into profit, so the target has to make sense.

When you pitch to throw your hat into the ring as a contributor, you want to follow all the pitching tips you learned about in the last chapter, like:

- Make it easy for them.
- Plan ahead.
- Don't be too promotional.
- Think of their audience first.

The two aspects I would add to keep in mind include not accepting any outside payment from anyone who wants to be included in your coverage and ensuring you get all ideas approved in advance to make the most out of your time.

Don't blow your media opportunity.

So many people I work with get nervous before they do an interview, especially a TV interview. I tell them all the same thing: *You're making a bigger deal about this in your head than it is in real life.*

Of course, it's easy for me to say this a TV reporter and anchor. Still, you need to ace this opportunity so it leads to many more.

There are seven things you need to keep in mind whenever you speak to a podcast host, reporter, or any other member of the media.

1. Know what you want to say.

If you don't know what you want to say, you'll end up talking too much and rambling. That's when you lose people. Go into the interview with talking points or bullet points so you can hit on what you want to say.

You also want to be sure you're answering the journalist's questions as well. Think of it like this: Question = Answer (+1). The Answer is your direct answer to the question. If you didn't get your talking point in, use that "+1" to segue into a talking point that drops a breadcrumb of your product or service. It could be as simple as, "And I talk more about that topic on my podcast, *Become a Media Maven.*"

2. Be conversational.

Don't memorize what you want to say. Yes, you want to know what you want to say, but remember, those are bullet points. You want to be conversational and not sound like a robot.

This makes for a much better interview, and it's more enjoyable for people to watch, read, or listen to.

3. Speak in sound bites or quotes.

Say what the journalist can't say. A journalist can tell you I'm a former TV reporter and anchor. I've worked in five different markets. That is what it is.

A journalist CAN'T share an animated story or two from my time in TV. Only I can do that, and only I can do it with emotion.

In a world of short form video content, think of a captivating twenty-second Instagram reel or YouTube short as a great sound bite.

4. Be animated.

You have to be animated for the same reason we wear more makeup and tease our hair bigger on TV. It's because things show up differently on camera, on-air, and even in print or online.

If you're talking to a journalist, he or she can hear your excitement and write to it. So make sure you get a little pep in your step before talking about your passion or expertise.

5. Ignore the camera.

It's a conversation. So many people play up the camera as a big and scary thing. They do the same thing with a microphone for a podcast or even just knowing they are doing an interview.

Block out the "media stuff" and focus on the conversation. I know it's easier said than done, but you need to try to get in that natural, likable space that will work for you.

6. Dress the part.

No, it doesn't always mean to dress up. If you're a chef, you should be in your apron. If you're a personal trainer, you should be in your workout gear. If you're a nurse or doctor, wear scrubs. If your brand color is red, wear red!

7. Don't overthink it.

Again, I know this is easier said than done, but no one knows how nervous you are, and honestly, they don't care. People are watching, listening, or reading your content for a reason, so be like Beyonce and put on your Sasha Fierce alter ego and just do the damn thing!

The key to nailing everything I outlined in this media training is to practice. Be a guest on podcasts. Host your own podcast. Record Instagram stories or reels. Have a friend or colleague interview you, record it, and have someone else give you feedback. But remember, don't take advice from someone who hasn't been where you're going.

Create a media kit.

Media kits aren't just for sales people to sell advertisements anymore. They are to sell you, your image, and your brand. I don't mean *sell* in the monetary meaning of the word—I mean sell yourself as an expert, an author, a speaker, the go-to person to choose when a media opportunity presents itself.

The media kit can come in a variety of forms. The most common is a PDF or a page on a website. While I used to love a pretty, branded PDF, I've become impartial to webpages. They're easier to share, update, and copy and paste when needed. Plus, you're not limited by length online.

Generally speaking, your media kit should include some of the following:

- Your name
- Your title
- Your unique selling point
- Your talking or speaking points
- Your headshot
- Your credibility (media attention/past speaking gigs)
- Your rates ("starting at" or a ballpark)
- Your website (if it's not there)
- Your social media handles
- Your audience reach
- Testimonials
- Your contact information

For an example of the media kit I use for media interviews and public speaking gigs, check out MediaMavenAndMore.com/bio. For another example as a blogger seeking sponsorships, log onto ChristinaAllDay.com/media-kit.

Both of these media kits serve different purposes, so they don't include the same information. Before you begin working on your media kit, be sure to have your goal in mind so you know what information is important to include.

Start landing public speaking gigs.

In 2018 I was invited to give a TEDx Talk in Boca Raton. It was titled "Fake News: It's Your Fault." (As you can imagine, it was a hot topic right before the election.)

You read that right. I was invited. I didn't apply like many speakers do.

So how did I get on the radar of the person planning the event? Someone who followed me on LinkedIn got to know about my expertise by seeing my posts. She was a volunteer at the event and told the organizer about me. That led to a lunch, a brainstorm of ideas, and I opened the event as the first speaker.

Since then, the video has earned more than one hundred thousand views and has led to paid speaking opportunities around the country.

That's one example of how you can leverage a talk to get paid to speak, but you don't need to stand in the red circle delivering a TED Talk to launch a speaking career or create an additional revenue stream.

But first, you need experience. Experience speaking on stage, or to a small group of people at a local chamber of commerce meeting, helps you perfect your talk and gives you the chance to bring along a photographer or videographer to create a reel.

Just like I taught you how to build a media list in the last chapter, we're going to start with a spreadsheet.

Head to your favorite search engine and type in either speaker, conference, or event + your industry or expertise + your city. You can also reach out to a local chamber of commerce or other local networking groups to see whether they accept outside speakers.

Other ways to find speaking opportunities are to read the trades and see if any conferences or events are mentioned in there. Ask your colleagues and clients about the events they attend. Reach out to local high schools and colleges if you have an angle that students can benefit from.

Also, don't be afraid to tell people you're a speaker. Add that term to your bio on social media and your resume. It's amazing how many people will see that, remember it, and refer you when something comes across their desk that may be a fit for you.

If all else fails, host your own event! It's so easy to do this virtually today.

While you're building your list of speaking opportunities, consider these seven things.

1. Start local. There are many groups looking for experts to educate their members.

2. Be creative and change your angle to reach as many people as possible.

3. Ask a friend for an introduction or pitching tips if they've been there and done that.

4. Join a local Toastmasters to hone your skills.

5. Search hashtags for events on social media. You can also use social media to find events and their organizers.

6. Don't worry about getting paid . . . yet. Build your experience and get feedback from listeners to get better.

7. You can still get paid. Share a call to action to build your email list, get on a call with someone, etc., so you can turn your delivery into dollars on the backend.

This is an example of an email I'd send to the leaders of networking groups or organizations:

Hi (insert name),

I'm writing to see if you accept outside speakers. If so, I'd love to hear your process for booking speakers for your audience.

Thanks.

Christina Nicholson

PS: For more on my expertise and delivery, click here to watch my recent TEDx Talk.

It's really that simple!

Take action.

I hope by now you've had a few quick wins if you've been taking action after each chapter.

Don't forget to download those sixteen places accepting contributors with story ideas and contact information at 16Places.com.

You can also map out what you will include in your media kit or speaker sheet since you're all set to pitch yourself!

6

TURN PUBLICITY INTO PROFIT

WHILE SOME PEOPLE do all this stuff to look cool on the internet, that's not you. Looking cool online doesn't pay the bills. Not directly, anyway. In this chapter, you're going to learn how to turn publicity into profit.

The biggest mistake people make after they earn media exposure, speak at an event, or get a contributor article published is to assume everyone saw it . . . so they do nothing. It shocks me how common this is. When the shock wears off, I get angry because so much money is being left on the table.

When I left TV news, I worked at a PR agency for six months before going off on my own to start Media Maven. At the agency, I worked with a man who created a baby product. His goal was to get his hands-free bottle-feeding product in front of moms.

As the account manager, I targeted all the national daytime talk shows, but because those were the big pie-in-the-sky goals, I also focused on smaller and niched outlets, including local TV and a variety of websites.

After earning coverage here and there, the big one finally hit. It was the *Rachael Ray Show*. It aired shortly before Mother's Day and was part of a Human Lab segment that showcased moms testing three different baby products.

Unfortunately, the producer of the segment never gave me a heads up this was running, so I found out about this major hit when my client called me to tell me, "We were just on *Rachael Ray*."

After that, my client applied to be on *Shark Tank*. The application is nearly twenty pages long. One part of that application includes a space to enter media attention you've earned for your business. Obviously, all the local, regional, and national media hits are impressive to show producers.

The creator of the product appeared as the first contestant on the first episode of season 7. He ended up making a deal with Lori Greiner and guest shark Ashton Kutcher.

Shortly after that, the product was available in big-box stores like Walmart and buybuy Baby. A few years later, it was acquired by a major company.

That's just one example of how publicity can turn into profit organically over a series of months.

Most of the time, you will have a snowball effect if you stick with pitching for months at a time. Very rarely will you have a one-hit wonder, and if you do, it will be short-lived. That's not to say that you can't see profit right after publicity.

One of my favorite clients at Media Maven was Little Words Project. Over the period of two years, we were successful in earning the original one-word bracelet local, regional, and national coverage, in addition to landing impressive media coverage for the founder of the company.

Coupled with a few roundup segments on the *TODAY Show*, the founder's story was featured in a segment called "She Made It." The story told her entrepreneurial journey as well as showcasing the beautiful product.

As you can imagine, the *TODAY Show*'s audience is a perfect target for inspirational bracelet stacks. That day and the days that followed, the company was slammed with orders and saw a huge bump in their Instagram followers.

So, yes, you can appear somewhere one day and see a profit on the same day. However, this is extremely rare. What's worse is that many people think this is the norm.

Do PR on your PR.

It's so important to do PR on your PR. This does so much more than just make the media hit live longer.

For example, when you share it on social media, it confirms to your followers that you are an expert in your industry. If they were on the fence about working with you before, they are more likely to move toward closing the deal because of your increased authority and credibility.

Sharing on social media is just one thing you can do after you earn exposure. Here are thirty-five other things you can do with your media hit:

1. Repeatedly share on social media. Don't share just one time.

There are so many reasons you need to share the exposure you've earned multiple times. First, you have an algorithm that is different for everybody, so you can't assume people see what you post.

If they do see it, it's safe to assume that in a few weeks they have forgotten about it because they've seen so many other things since then.

Finally, people who just started following most likely won't know where you featured a week, a month, or a year ago. For that reason, you need to show them.

For this, I use Agorapulse. The software makes it super easy to set it and forget it.

2. Amplify via paid social.

This is where the best of both worlds can come together. Not only do you get the authority and credibility through earned media, but you can control who sees it and when they see it by putting some ad spend behind it after it's published.

3. Tag the journalist and outlet when you share so they notice.

As more focus is put on tracking link clicks, letting a journalist know you are sharing the story they covered by tagging them is the ultimate way to say thank you. By doing this, they are more likely to come back to you for future stories that you may be a fit for.

Plus, when you tag a journalist in the story you share on social media, you make it easy for them to click or tap one button to share it with their audience.

4. Give anyone else mentioned in your article a social media shout-out.

In addition to tagging the journalist, tag the media outlet and any other sources mentioned in the coverage. This will drive more clicks, likes, and shares, amplifying your social proof.

5. Add it to a press page on your website.

Because social media is a constantly moving feed, it's important to keep all media hits and track press coverage in one place. A page dedicated to this on your website lets any potential customers or clients view it at any time.

6. Repurpose it into a video to post on social media or a blog.

I'm all about saving time by not reinventing the wheel. You can easily turn a video into a graphic or text or turn text into a graphic or video using tools like Canva. This gives the same thing a different look that increases your opportunity to share it even more.

7. Create a sizzle reel.

When you have a few different images, graphics, video, and text, put it together into one video to show your authority. This can live on your website, serve as content you post on social media, and be posted on your YouTube channel. I've even seen speakers use a sizzle reel as their introduction before they walk on stage.

8. This can be used as the perfect cover photo for your social media pages.

At a glance, this image being front and center will make you stand out from your competition. Remember, a picture is worth a thousand words.

9. Put the link in your email signature.

When you email potential customers and clients, this is a great way to give them a chance to see why you're the person to work with.

10. Insert media quotes into your company's bio or on your website's About page.

Curious readers can then see firsthand the publicity you have gained as a result of your expertise when they read your content.

11. Summarize an essential point made in the article to create additional content.

Just like mixing earned and paid media in the second point, you can do the same for owned and paid media. I'm a strong believer that every business owner should be creating content, and when you mention previous media coverage in your content creation, you're showcasing a positive reputation in another, new way.

12. Spark a debate or note how this example is a best practice and offers a solution to a recurring problem or situation.

Use the media coverage to start a conversation in the comments among your followers.

13. Encourage employees and happy customers to comment on the earned media itself.

Again, this tactic helps to keep the conversation going and draws more attention to the earned media. Additionally, employees' and customers' positive comments validate the work your company does.

Sending an email to your list sharing the coverage and asking for reactions online is a great way to jump-start this initiative.

14. Screenshot your media coverage as it shows up on search engines.

This serves as literal proof of how successful the earned media is. Post the screenshots on your website to show how the media coverage appeared on Google, Bing, Yahoo, etc. Sharing media successes helps build an unofficial resume, showing potential clients why they should do business with you.

15. Use "As Seen On" logos on marketing materials like your website, brochures, etc.

Those who want to appear as experts in relation to their niche will often look out for chances to be interviewed then use a logo such as the NBC peacock to show their media pickups, gaining credibility and prestige.

If the coverage is online, hyperlink the logo to the coverage so when people click, they can go straight to the story.

16. Add memorable quotes to your website to highlight your credibility.

Memorable quotes from media coverage can act as testimonials for your company, thus proving your validity.

17. Frame the placements.

Display your media coverage in your company's office where customers can see it while you remind them of your success. This also boosts morale among employees.

It will give your clients and potential customers confidence in your company.

18. Put them out during trade shows and relevant events.

Bring those framed placements mentioned above or make a large poster highlighting the media hits to give instant credibility and build desire. You can also create a portfolio full of coverage and bind glossy prints together to serve as a lookbook.

19. Use earned media in sales presentations to retailers.

This demonstrates the marketing muscle behind the brand. Instead of you telling people you're great, show them other people think you're great.

20. Mention it in some future pitches to prove credibility and authority.

Often local and regional earned media is all it takes to entice national and international media. Many media outlets will look to others for ideas on what to cover. This is where the snowball effect starts.

21. Ensure systems and processes are set up to respond quickly and efficiently to coverage reactions.

Is someone by the phone? Are you in your DMs to respond to messages? Is your lead magnet on your website set up to collect new email addresses? If not, you are not capturing leads from the attention you just earned.

22. Take your favorite hits from the month and do a top three review on a blog.

Some hits are better than others, and we want to champion those. Plus, this gives you an opportunity to rank for some keywords and drive people to your website.

23. Create an ebook or white paper of key points from the coverage.

In this content, add social media links and websites that go back to the media hit.

24. Use those traditional media hits to earn exposure in new media, like a podcast.

When you have coverage in one place on a certain medium, see how you can expand on that coverage to go deeper on a point in another outlet or form of media.

25. Mention the media hit in a newsletter.

I've recently become a big fan of newsletters and started sending my own every Thursday. It's a great way to keep people who subscribe in the loop of your expertise and the media coverage you're earning that doubles down on your knowledge.

26. Perhaps add some context, complemented by a photo or graphic, to underscore certain aspects of the subject that were not fully addressed in the article.

When you add anecdotes, images, video, or additional thoughts, you can repurpose the media hit in a variety of places and keep the conversation going with an additional angle.

27. Include the press coverage in blogs and email blasts.

This method is just a matter of hyperlinking to the earned coverage. Not only does this showcase your authority, but it also helps the journalist and their platform by giving them a backlink, so be sure to tell them about how you're sharing it.

28. Send great media hits to existing and prospective vendors, customers, and clients.

Again, this is a perfect example of someone else vouching for you and what you do instead of you telling others you're talented.

29. Turn the earned media into a pitch to become a sought-after paid speaker or land a book deal by connecting with trade organizations or literary agents.

One of the biggest factors in getting a book deal is having an audience, and earning media attention is something many publishers look for as a sign that your expertise is validated. Plus, there is so much overlap between getting press coverage and being a sought-after speaker. They are all paramount to having a recognizable personal brand.

30. Capitalize on the earned media to garner brand endorsements.

After one of my Media Mentoring Program clients was on TV, she was contacted by local food brands who wanted to sponsor inclusion on her blog. That's because they assumed she was already an influencer after her first TV appearance. Yes, it can happen that fast!

31. Create a Bitly or Pretty link to shorten the article's long URL so you can identify how many people click on the link to read the article on your end.

Tracking where your traffic comes from is vital in learning where your most engaged audience is. It gives you guidance on what's working and what's not so you make better marketing decisions in the future. Plus, those stats are something you can include in future pitches.

32. If there are appropriate industry blogs, reach out to those bloggers to suggest a post as a guest writer or arrange an interview and become a contributor.

Showing you've earned coverage in another place proves you are someone with clout in that niche, and it will increase your chances of earning even more attention online.

33. Conduct an interview with a source in the article and record a podcast or video that can be posted and shared on their end.

This is another way to repurpose the content with a different angle to make it not only live longer but also be shared more widely.

34. Reach out to everyone: current contacts, prospective clients, professional colleagues, industry peers, reporters, bloggers, potential collaborators, website visitors, event and conference attendees, LinkedIn, etc. to make the most of your media coverage.

Don't think you're oversharing. Nine times out of ten, people will be happy for you and impressed, and the more you do this, the less likely they are to forget about you and what you do.

35. Mail hard copies of coverage to past, present, and prospective clients.

There's just something about having a physical copy, isn't there?

Take action.

This is where many people fail to act because they assume the coverage is enough. By now, you know that's not true.

Create a plan on what to do after you earn press. I always jump into my social media scheduler and post it as a recurring evergreen post. Then, I head to my website and link to it on my press page.

What's your plan going to be?

7

———

YOU CAN (AND SHOULD) ALWAYS GO HOME

I'VE TOUCHED on content creation a bit in the last few chapters, but now, I'm going to go deep as it relates to creating content for your website.

It's so important to have a website as your home base. Not just because you are in control of the content and narrative but also because it is the perfect place to send someone after they first hear of you online, on TV, or on a podcast.

Your homepage.

Your website should answer these three questions right away:

1. What do I offer?
2. How will it make your life better?
3. What do you need to do to get it?

This is not the time to try to be cute and clever. Instead, be very clear so there is no confusion.

One of the reasons Costco is so successful is because the store makes it so easy for people to buy things by eliminating confusion. It does this by offering only one or two options of a product. Unlike at a grocery store, you won't see five different brands of the same thing. That's when people stop, think, and get decision fatigue.

You also want to include an obvious call to action. Instead of saying "learn more" or "get started," show you believe in your product or service by asking for the sale. Make your button say "Download now" or "Subscribe" or "Buy in bulk."

While you're answering those three questions, try to go deeper and make people think about more than just the problem you solve. Point out what could happen if they *don't* buy from you.

Now, do the opposite of what I just mentioned and tell your website visitor what success will look like if they work with you or purchase your product.

Then, share a plan. Show people how easy it is to do business with you. It can be as simple as:

Step 1: Jewelry is selected.

Step 2: Jewelry is created.

Step 3: Jewelry is shipped to you.

Finally, something that should be on your homepage is a way to capture the visitor's email address. There should be a free resource they get in exchange for their email address.

Everything else that you thought was important—like your About page, FAQ, blog, etc.—should be linked in the footer. When it's at the top, it takes away from the main purpose of your website, which is to convert visitors into customers or clients.

SEO.

I could get into technical SEO here, but I'm not going to. That is not my expertise, but I do know some basics like make sure your images are compressed, ensure your website is mobile friendly, eliminate plug-ins you don't use, and have a fast load time.

I have fun with SEO when it's in the form of creating content on a regular basis. The best way to do this is to have a blog page where you add a new post on a weekly basis, at least.

When blogging started in the early 2000s, people were blogging for the sake of blogging. Today, things are different. You need to have an SEO-focused strategy with the research to back it up so your blog is found in search engines.

I was originally turned onto blogging for SEO by Brandon Gaille, the host of the *Blogging Millionaire* podcast. He is also the founder of RankIQ, software that helps bloggers rank while taking things into account that many other software programs do not.

For example, I could focus on a specific keyword phrase, but if all the websites currently ranking for that same keyword phrase have a higher domain authority than mine, then there is little chance my post with outrank theirs.

The purpose of a blog is to drive traffic to your website and showcase you and your brand as the go-to service or product in your niche. Having a blog is a great way to consistently update your website, land contributing roles, and book speaking gigs, and it serves as the perfect place to insert a relevant call to action.

The key to being found online through your blog is to focus on keyword phrases with low competition. While this is not a fast strategy, it is one that works overtime.

Creating content.

In chapter 4, I talked about the importance of timing when pitching the media. The same rules apply for content creation.

My personal favorite rule that applies to this is planning ahead. As a reminder, you work backward from the days in the calendar to write for the future. This could be both writing a blog post for your website and writing an article to contribute to another website.

When you have those relevant awareness days, holidays, and seasons marked in your calendar, it's time to schedule your SEO keyword research, content creation, and promotion.

First, start with your list of keywords and keyword phrases. You want these to have low competition and plan to make the post or article better than those currently ranking for the keywords or keywords phrases.

To do this, you will most likely need to rely on software. Again, my favorite for keyword research is RankIQ.

After you have batched a spreadsheet of keywords and keywords phrases, you can begin writing your first post. I like to use AI to get me started. Then, I go back through and add personal stories and my personality in the draft. Most of the time, I also add a variety of sections to make the post longer and more in depth than others currently ranking.

When it's written and published, it's time to promote it. I use Agorapulse to schedule a tease to the blog post and link on social media. Some other ways to share it are creating a pin and sharing it on Pinterest, mentioning it on a podcast, and linking to it in a newsletter.

Make sure you include a call to action in your blog post when it's relevant. You can do this in the text, by adding a button in between paragraphs, or even just by ensuring the footer on each page of your website features the opportunity to opt into your lead magnet.

Time block and batch.

I like to create content by time blocking and batching. By doing this, you significantly improve productivity and efficiency.

Time blocking allows you to allocate specific blocks of time to focus on creating content without distractions. By setting aside dedicated periods for content creation, you can minimize interruptions and maintain a concentrated mindset without distractions.

When you allocate specific time slots for content creation, you create a structured framework that helps you stay on track and complete tasks efficiently. The clear boundaries set by time blocking can motivate you to make the most of the allocated time and accomplish more within each session.

By incorporating this practice into your routine, you develop a habit of regularly producing content and avoid procrastination or inconsistency.

By predetermining when you will work on content creation, you eliminate the need to make constant decisions about when to start or stop. This reduces decision fatigue, freeing up mental energy for the actual creative process.

Time blocking enables you to effectively manage your time by creating a visual representation of your schedule. By allocating specific time slots for different content creation activities, such as brainstorming, writing, editing, and publishing, you gain a clearer understanding of how your time is used and can optimize it accordingly.

So now that we've blocked time off in our calendar, this is why you should batch everything you do at once.

When applied to content creation, it allows you to focus on one type of activity, such as writing or recording, for an extended period. This minimizes context switching, reduces distractions, and improves workflow efficiency.

Batching provides an opportunity to get into a creative flow state. By immersing yourself in a specific type of content creation activity, you can deepen your focus, improve idea generation, and produce higher-quality content.

When you batch content creation tasks, you can streamline your processes and develop efficient workflows. For example, if you are recording videos, you can set up your recording equipment once and then record multiple videos in a single session, saving time and effort.

Batching allows you to save time by minimizing the work required for setup, context switching, and transitioning between different types of content creation activities. By eliminating unnecessary breaks and interruptions, you can complete tasks more quickly and dedicate additional time to other aspects of your work.

Batching encourages consistency in content creation. By dedicating specific time blocks to batched activities, such as writing multiple blog posts or creating a series of social media graphics, you can build a backlog of content, maintain a regular publishing schedule, and ensure a steady flow of output.

Remember, we're doing a lot here. Just look at how much you've learned so far. To put this into action, you need to be smart with how you spend your time, and time blocking and batching will help.

To save time, you can also repurpose your long-form blog post or article to create other content for different platforms. Here are some examples:

1. Tweak the headline text in your social media post each time you link to the article. For example, you could pull out the quotes, ask a question, or tease to a tangible takeaway.
2. If the blog post performs well, turn it into a YouTube video. Chances are, it'll do well there too.
3. Turn it into a podcast episode or a pitch to be a guest on a popular podcast.
4. Turn it into a graphic or a video for an Instagram reel or TikTok.
5. Tweak it to post as an article on LinkedIn.
6. Tweak it to submit as a contributed post.
7. Turn it into a Twitter/X thread or LinkedIn post.
8. Create an ebook or whitepaper.
9. Turn it into an infographic.
10. Screenshot images of the tweet/post or Twitter/X thread and turn them into social media posts.

I'm touching on social media a bit here but will stop now. That's what we will dive into in the next chapter!

Take action.

If you haven't already, it's time to take an audit of your current website and blog. Make some changes as you see fit.

I also want you to create a blogging schedule and put it in your calendar. When it's in the calendar, you have to stick to it!

8

LET'S GET SOCIAL

WE'VE all heard those amazing social media stories of Justin Bieber and Halle Bailey being discovered by Usher and Beyoncé because they posted videos of themselves singing on YouTube.

Then there is Jax with her Victoria's Secret hit she sang on TikTok. Speaking of TikTok, Addison Rae brought in tens of millions of dollars after she built a following dancing on the app.

I could go on, but you get the point.

However, this is not a book about social media. I don't think those age too well. Instead, this book is about how to become a Media Maven, and you can do that using social media to amplify your voice and your pitch to the media. Here's how.

What we pay attention to.

Today, you're more likely to pay attention to a notification on social media than you are another email in your inbox. That's why I always suggest pinging the person you're pitching on social media before and after you pitch them.

For example, after I sent an email pitching online course creator Amy Porterfield to appear on CNN Headline News, I sent a tweet/post to the show anchor, producer, and booker letting them know I just sent a pitch via email about the topic.

Again, with a full inbox, people are more likely to pay attention to a Twitter/X notification than an email notification, especially if they are a producer and not forward-facing like a podcast host or news anchor.

Why Twitter/X? Generally speaking, this is the social media platform where members of the media are most active.

Before I get into some social media 101 and 102, I want to emphasize the importance of connecting with these people *before* you send a ping like this. Not only will this help give you a better idea of what interests them by seeing their tweets/posts and promotion of their own articles, segments, or shows, but it will also prove you're not following them and interacting with them just to be self-serving.

What should I post?

If you're like me, you may hop over to a business's Facebook page and assume they've gone out of business if they haven't posted in a few months. You don't want people to have this perception of you and your business, so it's important to have a presence on the outlets your clients or customers are active on.

There are five types of posts you can pull inspiration from, and these are posts that inspire, educate, entertain, connect, and promote.

A post that inspires will make someone feel good. It could be a positive or motivational quote. Storytelling is huge on social media and often leads to increased engagement. You want to make the person consuming your content think and give them something to aspire to.

For nonfiction authors, public speakers, and those trying to build a personal brand, posts that educate are vital. This is where you will teach, offer value, give tips, share fun facts, answer frequently asked quotations, and even provide a mini training. Just like we covered in the previous pitching segments, get as granular and tangible as possible so people are learning something new and not the generic stuff we've all heard before.

Lots of people head to social media to be entertained, so this is where you want to grab a person's attention and keep it. You can do this by showing your humor and making them laugh, having fun with everyday situations, showing some behind-the-scenes content so they can experience something new with you. Video content is huge in entertainment.

People do business with people they know, like, and trust. That's where connection come into play. Tell a relatable story, be a little vulnerable and open up, share a silly or funny mistake that people can relate to.

Now, it's time to make all of that work for you in dollars. There is a reason I saved this one for last. If you don't start with everything I mentioned above, this kind of post will fall flat. After you've inspired, educated, entertained, and connected with your ideal customer or client, make sure they recognize what problems they're having and how you can help give them a solution. You want to make it easy for them to take the next steps with you.

Now, grab them and GROW.

How can I grab more attention with my content? How can I be real and authentic in my captions? What can I offer my audience that is of value? What is my *why*, and how can I share it to connect deeply?

That's what this section is all about and all you need to remember is how to GROW: Grab, Real, Offer, Why.

Let's start with the G in GROW, grab attention. To do this, use graphics, photos, and videos. Think of a headline like an article or tabloid would use. Use relevant hashtags. Use the caption to grab attention in the first two lines. Once you grab attention, keep it. Remember, people want to connect with you.

You have to be real. That's the R in GROW. Talk to your audience like you would a customer or friend. To do this, read the caption out loud to ensure it's brand appropriate. Keep your tone friendly and not robotic. Show behind the scenes for an extra human element. You can start with voice notes and turn that into a caption to sound more conversational. Share relatable stories to connect on a deeper level.

A nonnegotiable is offering value. That's the O in GROW. Make it obvious what is in it for them. Ensure you are sharing a hot topic that sparks conversation. Be a giver, overshare, and over deliver. Don't hold back thinking that's what will make people buy. Add value to your audience by solving a problem. Make people want to save and share your post . . . and write that in the post, too, so they act on it!

Now, let's finish with the W, sharing your why. Make it clear why you do what you do. Share images and videos that showcase your why. This is where people will really get to know, like, and trust you.

Making social simple.

Now, let's end this chapter with some tips on making this execution as simple as possible.

Batch the content based on your promotional calendar to save time.

Repeat evergreen posts every few month. Trust me, no one will notice.

Check and respond to notifications, like comments and messages, once a day.

Share content from potential partners.

Use social media management tools to schedule posts in advance. You can also manage notifications in these apps so doom scrolling isn't an issue.

See if a team member or virtual assistant is interested in managing your social media channels.

Use a resource like Canva to create images and videos. With tens of thousands of templates, it can be your shortcut to creating visual content.

Take action.

Something I do is schedule one hour a week to batch and schedule social media content. Decide what cadence you want to work with in your business and put it in your calendar so you're showing up on social media.

You can also use what you learned in this chapter to help you create a content calendar.

9
———

THAT WORD: INFLUENCERS

NATURALLY, I'm following up the social media chapter with this one. Influencers. I'm honestly not a big fan of that word, but for lack of a better one, we'll go with it.

Remember, I'm not going to teach you how to be an influencer. Again, that's another book for another person to write that may not age well because of the rapid changes in the industry. The purpose of this chapter is to teach you how to work with influencers to get them to talk about you because they are also "the media."

First, let's cover the basics.

Influencer dos and don'ts.

Don't ask for favors. If the influencer is not your BFF, they don't owe you a free promotion. Don't ask them to develop a story, create content, and promote it to their audience they spent time and money building.

What's in it for them? Are you paying them? Is it a trade for a product or service? Either way, put a value on it and ensure that value is put in writing and it is fair on both ends.

I'd like to go a little deeper on this and share a story of an experience with a client. The client was a med spa and did not want to pay influencers for social media promotion. Instead, they wanted to trade services like laser hair removal and Botox treatments.

While there is nothing wrong with that, the client was very particular about the influencers we approached. They did not want nano influencers (your everyday social media users, with anywhere from one hundred to ten thousand followers) and was very selective about microinfluencers (influencers with follower counts in the range of ten thousand to one hundred thousand followers).

The problem with this is the caliber of influencer they wanted to work with did not work for trades. The caliber of influencers they were targeting worked as influencers full-time so were past their days of trading services to take their business to the next level and were more than a $500 trade.

Keep this in mind when you build your media list of influencers.

Set expectations. You need a contract to determine deliverables, approval, timeline, results, and payment. Period.

What's your ROI? Remember, most of the time, this is for exposure, not sales. The sales are a bonus, so think of the short-term and long-term goals. For example, maybe it's a longer campaign or specific call to action, for example.

Ask for a referral. If you had a good experience, then ask for an introduction to another influencer they admire or ask someone else in your industry who they like.

Now that we've gotten that out of the way, let's go deeper.

The fakers.

You don't want to work with "influencers" who buy followers, are part of engagement pods, and won't get your product or service in front of the right people. Here are some things to pay attention to ensure you're not falling for the fakers and their tricks.

When it comes to how many followers or fans someone has, ignore the number. Anyone can buy followers on the internet. Some people increase their numbers by doing giveaways.

Engagement? Also take what you see here with a grain of salt. You can buy likes, views, comments, etc. too. If you are going to look at engagement, take a good look at the quality of engagement. You can usually tell by what people are responding with if they are truly interested or not.

These are the two things you should pay attention to: insights and audience.

Ask the influencer for a screenshot or video recording of their insights to get an idea of what's really happening behind the scenes in the app. Social media insights show information that helps businesses gain a deeper understanding of their audience by sharing their age range, gender, where they live, etc. Again, if the engagement is high, then take a peek at what's happening in the comments to ensure it's genuine.

If your audience is women in the USA, then you want to ensure your influencer has the same audience. This is another screenshot or video recording you're going to want to ask for to ensure they will help you reach the right people.

Approaching influencers.

Follow and engage. Don't come out of nowhere. Be an active member of their community.

Include them. Have them on your podcast, shout them out in a blog, tag them in a social media post.

Just ask. A simple question like, "Do you work with brands? I'd love to learn more about how you can help me get the word out about XYZ. Could you pass along your media kit?"

If you can't pay them, just wait. Advertising should always come last and not be a desperate attempt for sales. Remember, marketing is a long-term game. You can also get creative to try to make it work . . . or just become the niche influencer yourself!

For more resources on how to become an influencer yourself, learn from the best who have joined me on my podcast, *Become a Media Maven*. Some episodes include:

- "How to Become an Instagram Influencer in 9 Steps" with Christina Galbato
- "How to Make a Living as a Digital Content Creator" with Adaleta Avdic
- "How to Become an Influencer Entrepreneur" with Jenny Melrose

Take action.

Now, I want you to jump on your favorite social media app and find influencers who have your ideal customer or client. I'd imagine you're already following them, and if that's the case, start interacting with them. If you're not already, start commenting and let them know you're there and like what they're doing.

10

HOW MUCH?

BEFORE I LEAVE you with your marching orders to execute what you've learned so far, I want to share one thing you may encounter when you begin to put yourself out there and how to handle it.

People will ask for money. They will turn your editorial pitch into an invitation to purchase an advertisement. Like D.A.R.E. taught us in elementary school, just say no.

The scams in your DMs.

If I'm getting these scams in my DMs, then I'm going to guess you are too. When it comes to people sending you messages about opportunities that are too good to be true, please consider the source.

Nearly every time, the people promising to get you in certain publications are not affiliated with the publications. Even if they are, they cannot guarantee you coverage. Remember, the only way to guarantee coverage is by paying for an ad. Even then, you will have a contract by someone who is on the sales team at that specific media outlet with its reach, specifications, editorial calendar, audience demographics, and more.

Paying to play.

Then there are those tricky ways to get you to pay for ads, like all the councils at *Forbes* or the networks at *Entrepreneur*. They will say congratulations for getting the opportunity then will follow up by asking you to pay them to write for them. It's the opposite of a job.

I'm all about contributing to outlets when it builds your brand in front of your ideal customer or client, but this is different.

Not only is this advertising, but it's tricky advertising. Some sites aren't even part of the actual publication. Instead, their name is licensed. Because you're paying for this coverage, the backlinks are no-follow so you don't get the SEO.

Also, some journalists will think of you as less credible if you pay for coverage like this.

Because of this, people are paying contributors under the table for coverage, and many of these outlets are happy to have the content so they just turn a blind eye. But if it gets called out publicly, all those articles will disappear. I've seen it happen many times before.

I've also seen people pay money to so-called contributors, or people who work with contributors, and get nothing in return. Remember, you can't buy an ad from someone who isn't qualified to sell ads.

While these pay-to-play appearances could impress people who don't know any better, you're better off just working a tad harder to earn a contributing role at a popular outlet. Then when you do, leverage that and repurpose that content into even more.

Sometimes when you pitch for earned coverage, someone will respond and try to sell you an ad, but they sugar coat the term and call it an advertorial or sponsored article. Reiterate you're interested only in editorial coverage and ask them to keep you in mind.

If you want to contribute without pitching article ideas, try Thrive Global, Medium, or your own LinkedIn profile page.

Advertising.

If you are going to advertise, be clear on what your goal is. What do you want people to do when they see the ad? Keep it in mind from start to finish.

Also, focus on a freebie or lead magnet. It's hard to go from an ad to a sale directly. Instead, warm up the audience and go from advertisement to something free.

All advertising should be tracked with numbers. If not, you won't know what works and what doesn't. Digital is best for this.

Don't forget who your ideal customer or client is during the advertising process.

The more niche, the more likely you'll see an ROI. Remember my client with the running app? The niche magazine and website *Runner's World* was a more successful media hit than the more popular *TODAY Show*.

I'm also a big fan of social media advertising because it's easy to do so many things on your own and drill down on a variety of tasks to get the most bang for your buck.

For example, you can target by specific location, likes, website visitors, people similar to your website visitors, etc.

It's so easy to start small and work your way up once you see people responding to certain ads. Not only can you test this way, but you can also tweak the images, videos, and ad copy at any time.

You can see exactly what works and what doesn't in real time.

Take action.

This is where you remember to do your research. Don't believe something that sounds too good to be true. Consider the source.

Also, not all advertising is bad. For example, I'm a fan of sponsoring newsletters, but have never had a lot of luck with Instagram or Facebook ads. When you have a budget, focus on ROI when ad dollars are being spent.

11

KNOWLEDGE IS POTENTIAL POWER—NOW, LET'S MAKE THIS POWERFUL AF

CONGRATULATIONS! You've reached the final chapter of this book, and by doing so, you've shown a commitment to professional growth. By now, you've acquired valuable knowledge, insights, and ideas.

Now, what are you going to do with it?

The importance of executing what you've learned cannot be overstated. Knowledge is potential power. It's up to you to make it powerful now.

In today's fast-paced world, we are bombarded with information from various sources—books, articles, podcasts, online courses, and more.

While reading can be an excellent way to expand our understanding, it can also become an endless cycle of consumption without implementation. We're all guilty of this.

This final chapter serves as a reminder to break free from that cycle and give you a kick in the ass to make shit happen!

Before taking action, take a moment to reflect on what you have read here. Consider the key concepts, ideas, and lessons that resonated with you the most. What are the insights that have the potential to make a significant impact on your business? Identifying these points will help you prioritize your actions and ensure you focus on what truly matters.

To effectively execute what you've learned, it is essential to set clear, actionable goals. Break down the larger concepts into smaller, manageable tasks that align with your vision. By doing so, you will create a roadmap that guides your actions and allows for measurable progress.

Start with a single step. Don't let the fear of imperfection or uncertainty hold you back from taking action. Start small but start now. The first step is often the most challenging, but it is also the most crucial.

As you put your knowledge into action, remember it is an iterative process. Embrace the concept of continuous improvement and be open to adapting your approach as you learn and grow. Don't be discouraged by setbacks or failures. Instead, view them as valuable lessons that provide opportunities for refinement and progress.

Accountability can significantly enhance your commitment to execution. Find an accountability partner, join a mastermind group, or share your goals with a trusted friend or mentor. By involving others in your journey, you create a support system that keeps you motivated, focused, and on track.

Regularly evaluate your progress and assess the effectiveness of your actions. Are you moving closer to your goals? What adjustments can you make to improve your execution? Be honest with yourself and be willing to make necessary changes. Flexibility and adaptability are key to long-term success.

Along your journey of executing what you've learned, don't forget to celebrate your wins and milestones, no matter how small they may seem. Recognize your achievements, acknowledge your growth, and use these celebrations as fuel to keep pushing forward. As business owners, we get in the habit of moving the goalpost as soon as hit a goal. Try not to do that.

As you experience the positive outcomes of executing what you've learned, consider sharing your knowledge and experiences with others. Pay it forward by mentoring someone, leading a workshop, or writing about your journey. I'd be grateful if you share this book with them, recommend my podcast, or send people to my newsletter.

Remember, the true value in what you've read lies in putting that knowledge into action. Embrace the principles outlined in this final chapter. The possibilities are endless when you combine knowledge with action.

RESOURCES

This doesn't have to be goodbye. Sure, you finished the book, but wait . . . there's more.

Listen to my podcast, *Become a Media Maven*, in your favorite podcast app.

Get more media and publicity tips, tricks, and strategies sent to your inbox once a week by joining my newsletter at **Media-MavenAndMore.com/newsletter**.

Spend less than an hour learning the 5 simple steps to getting featured in the media without spending money on ads. **This masterclass is FREE at EarnMediaNow.com**

In three hours, I'll teach you how to pitch the media to earn publicity and turn it into profit. **Join my bootcamp now at MediaMavenAndMore.com/publicity.**

Are you ready to bring PR in-house? **In my Media Mentoring Program at MediaMentoringProgram.com**, you or a VA can learn how to become a publicist with the skills of a big PR agency.

ACKNOWLEDGMENTS

I'd like to acknowledge my husband, Colin Nicholson, for doing everything for me and our three kids, Julianna, Landon, and Dylan.

I would not have known what to do throughout this book writing process without the help of fellow authors Anna David, Melanie Herschorn, and Laura Briggs.

Lisa Simone Richards, thanks for being my weekly account-ability partner so I could finally get this damn thing done.

ABOUT THE AUTHOR

Christina Nicholson started her decade-long career as a TV reporter and anchor. That took her from Columbus, Ohio, to New York City to Beaumont, Texas (where she met her husband at a country bar), to Fort Myers, Florida, and to the other coast of Florida where her full-time TV career finally came to an end in the Miami and Fort Lauderdale area.

After leaving TV news, Christina started her PR agency, Media Maven, where she and her team of women help businesses of all sizes earn exposure in the media without spending money on ads.

She is also the host of the Become A Media Maven podcast and the founder of Podcast Clout, a podcast database that makes it easy for thought leaders and PR professionals to build podcast pitch lists of the current top, relevant podcasts.

She has been awarded and named an Up & Comer by *South Florida Business & Wealth* magazine, Best PR Blogger and Social Media Campaign by the Gold Coast PR Council, Above & Beyond Social Media Recognition by NBC, and the Green Eyeshade Award for breaking news coverage.

In 2018 she stood in the red circle on the TEDx stage in Boca Raton and delivered a talk titled "Fake News: It's Your Fault" that has more than one hundred thousand views.

As a regular contributor to multiple online outlets, you can read her work in Huff Post, Thrive Global, Inc. Magazine, Business

Insider, Fast Company, Today Parents, and Boss Babe. You can still see her in front of the camera as a TV host on Lifetime TV, a producer and field correspondent on Health Uncensored with Dr. Drew, and on other local and national TV networks.

In addition to having a local lifestyle and family blog, Christina All Day, Christina is an avid reader and book lover with her own Little Free Library.

She lives in Wellington, Florida, with her husband and three young children where she can't get enough pepperoni pizza and chicken nachos and downs a Coke day. (She knows it's a bad habit, but it's just too good to break!)

URGENT PLEA!

Thank you for reading my book!

I really appreciate all of your feedback and I love hearing what you have to say. I need your input to make the next version of this book and my future books better.

Please take two minutes now to leave a helpful review on Amazon letting me know what you thought of the book: MediaMavenAndMore.com/review

Thanks so much!
—Christina

FREE GIFT

To get the best experience with this book, I've found readers who download and use "The Exact Pitch" are able to implement faster and take the next steps needed to become a regular on TV, on podcasts, in print, and online.

You can get a copy by visiting:
www.TheExactPitch.com